THE SHOE FOR YOUR LEFT FOOT
WON'T FIT ON YOUR RIGHT

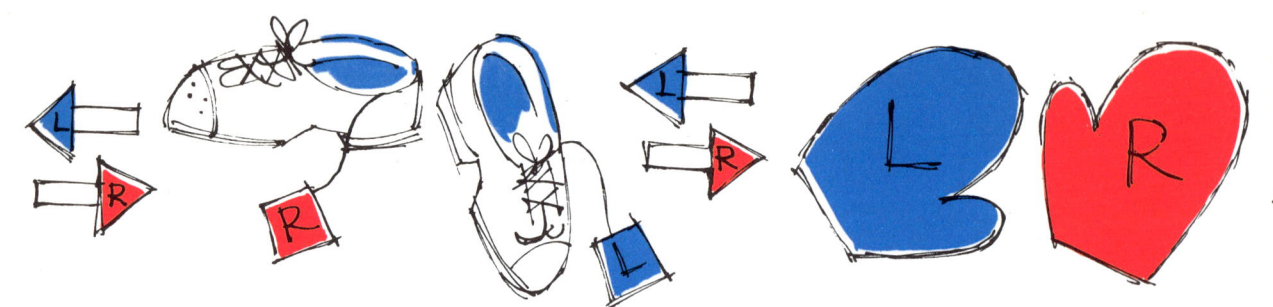

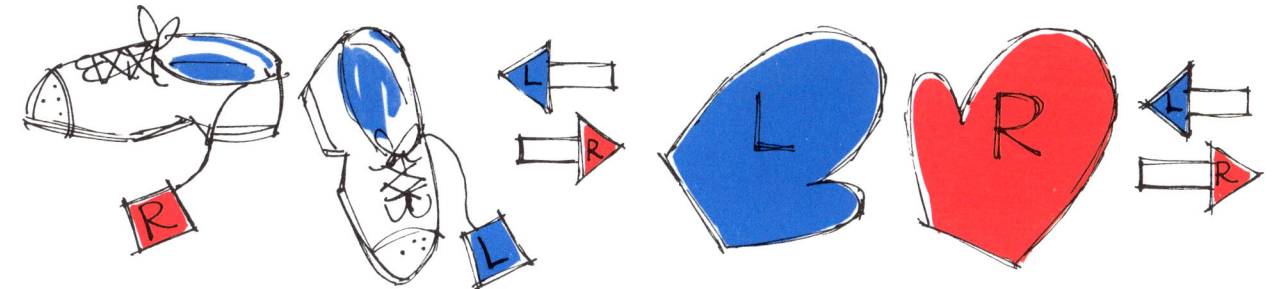

THE SHOE FOR YOUR LEFT FOT
WON'T FIT ON YOUR RIGHT

BY ROZ ABISCH
ILLUSTRATED BY BOCHE KAPLAN

The McCall Publishing Company · New York

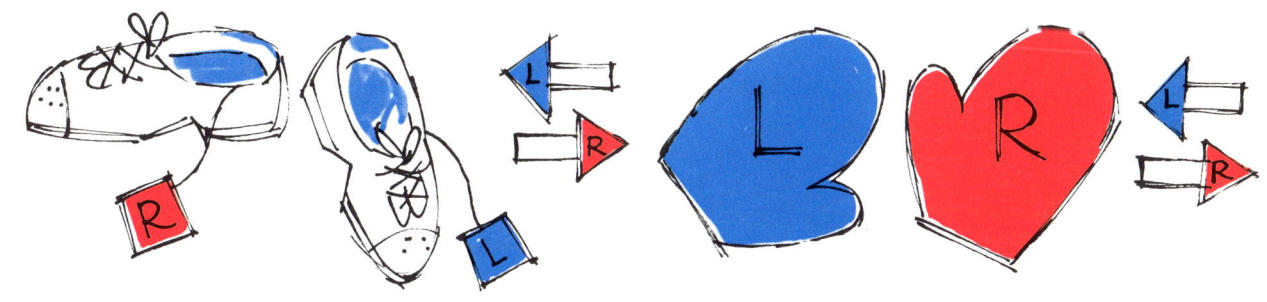

Do you know how to tell left from right?
Start with your hands.
This is your left hand.

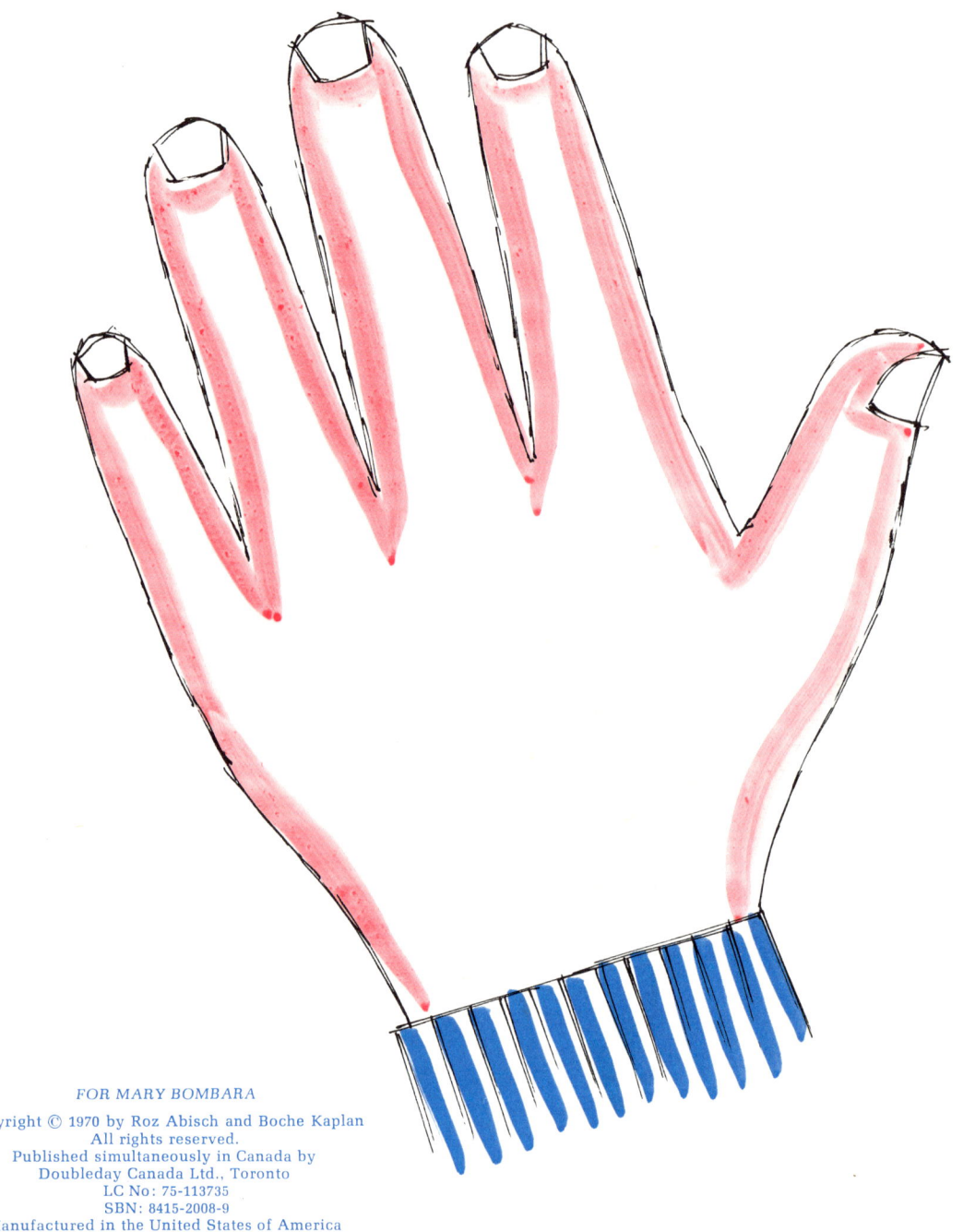

FOR MARY BOMBARA

Copyright © 1970 by Roz Abisch and Boche Kaplan
All rights reserved.
Published simultaneously in Canada by
Doubleday Canada Ltd., Toronto
LC No: 75-113735
SBN: 8415-2008-9
Manufactured in the United States of America

This is your right hand.

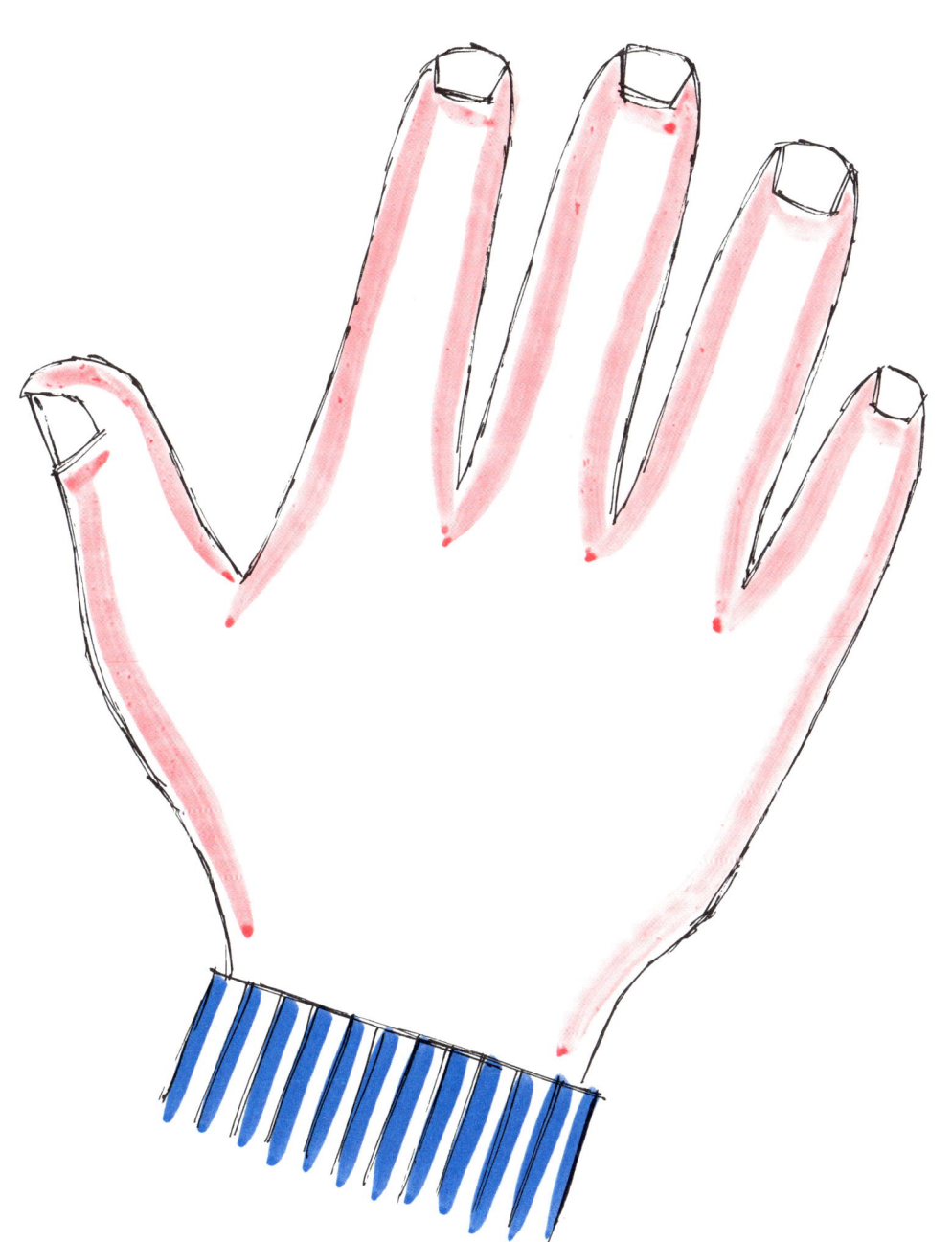

Look at your shoes.
They are different.
One shoe is for your left foot.
The other is for your right foot.

The shoe for your left foot won't fit on the right.
Which is your left foot?
Which is your right foot?

From the top of your head,
down to the tip of your toes,
this is your left side.

This is your right side.

Now, stand side by side.
The person near your left side stands
on your left.

The person near your right side stands *on your right.*

To salute our flag, place your right hand across to the left side of your chest over your heart.

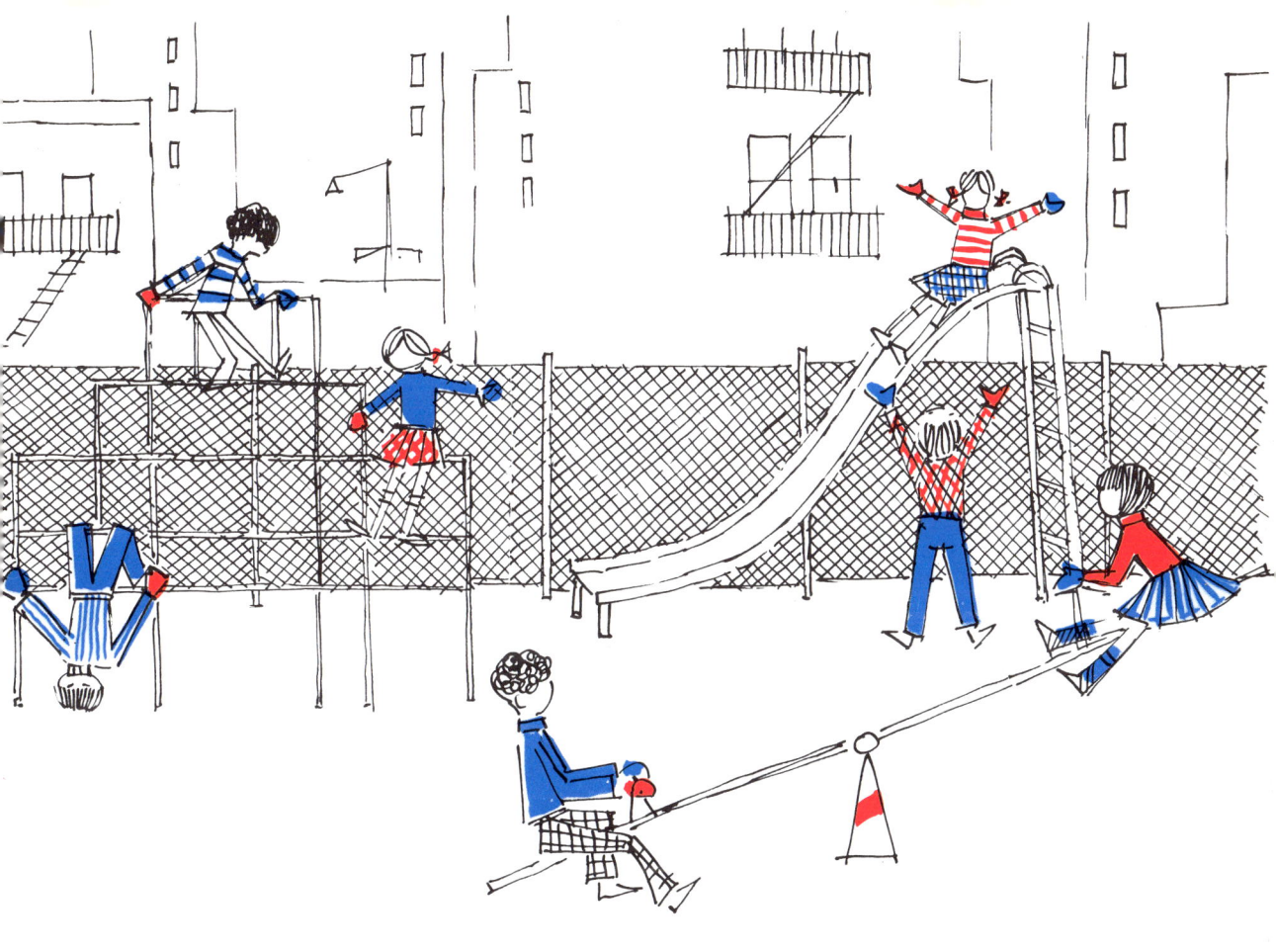

When grownups greet each other, they always shake hands with their right hand.

Some people write with their left hand.
They eat with their left hand.
They hold a scissors in their left hand.
People who do most things with their left hand
are *left-handed.*
But there are more *right-handed* people than
left-handed people.
Which hand do you use to throw a ball?

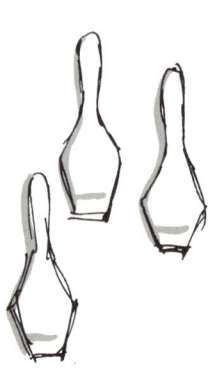

Which hand do you use to hold a spoon?
Are *you* left-handed or right-handed?

If anything lines up or moves
in this direction
we say it goes *from left to right.*

On the calendar the days of the week
go from left to right.

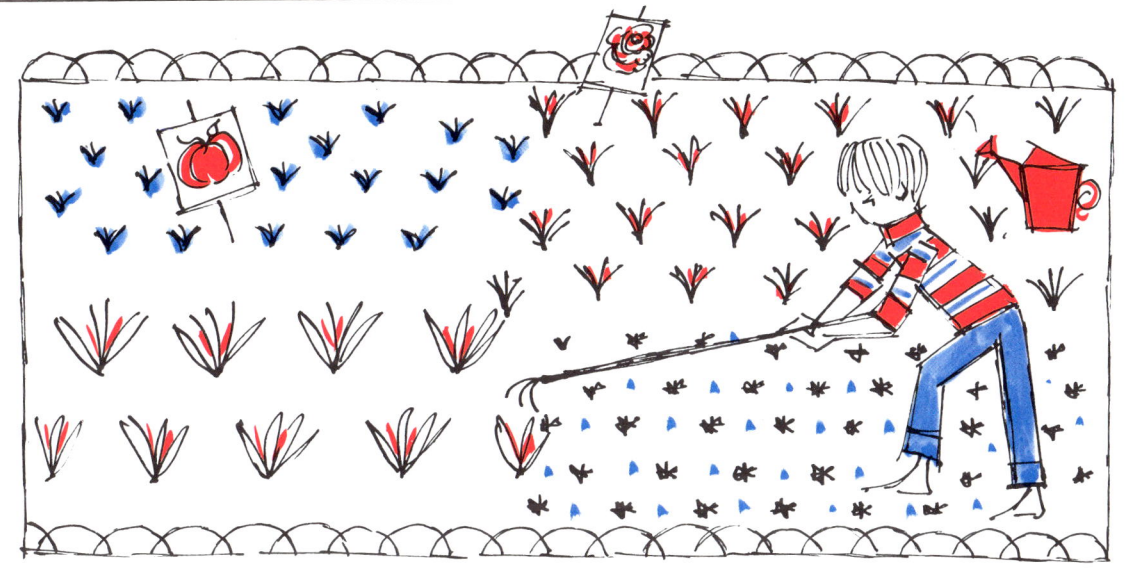

MAY

SUNDAY	MONDAY	TUESDAY	WEDNESDAY	THURSDAY	FRIDAY	SATURDAY
		1	2	3	4	5
6	7	8	9	10	11	12
13	14	15	16	17	18	19
20	21	22	23	24	25	26
27	28	29	30	31		

Every book has a left side and a right side.

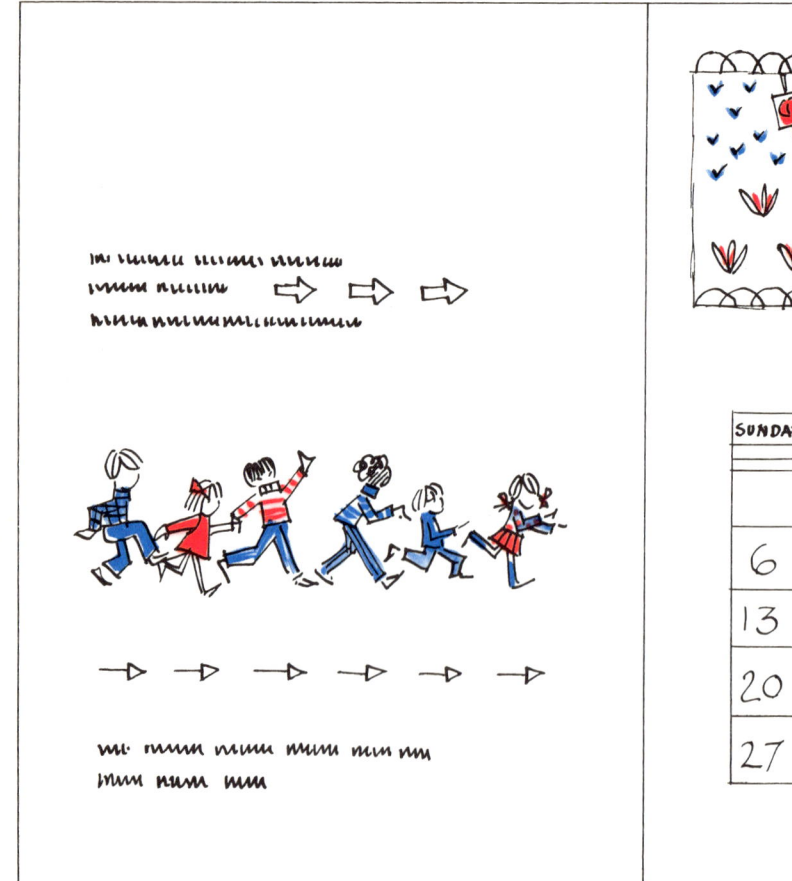

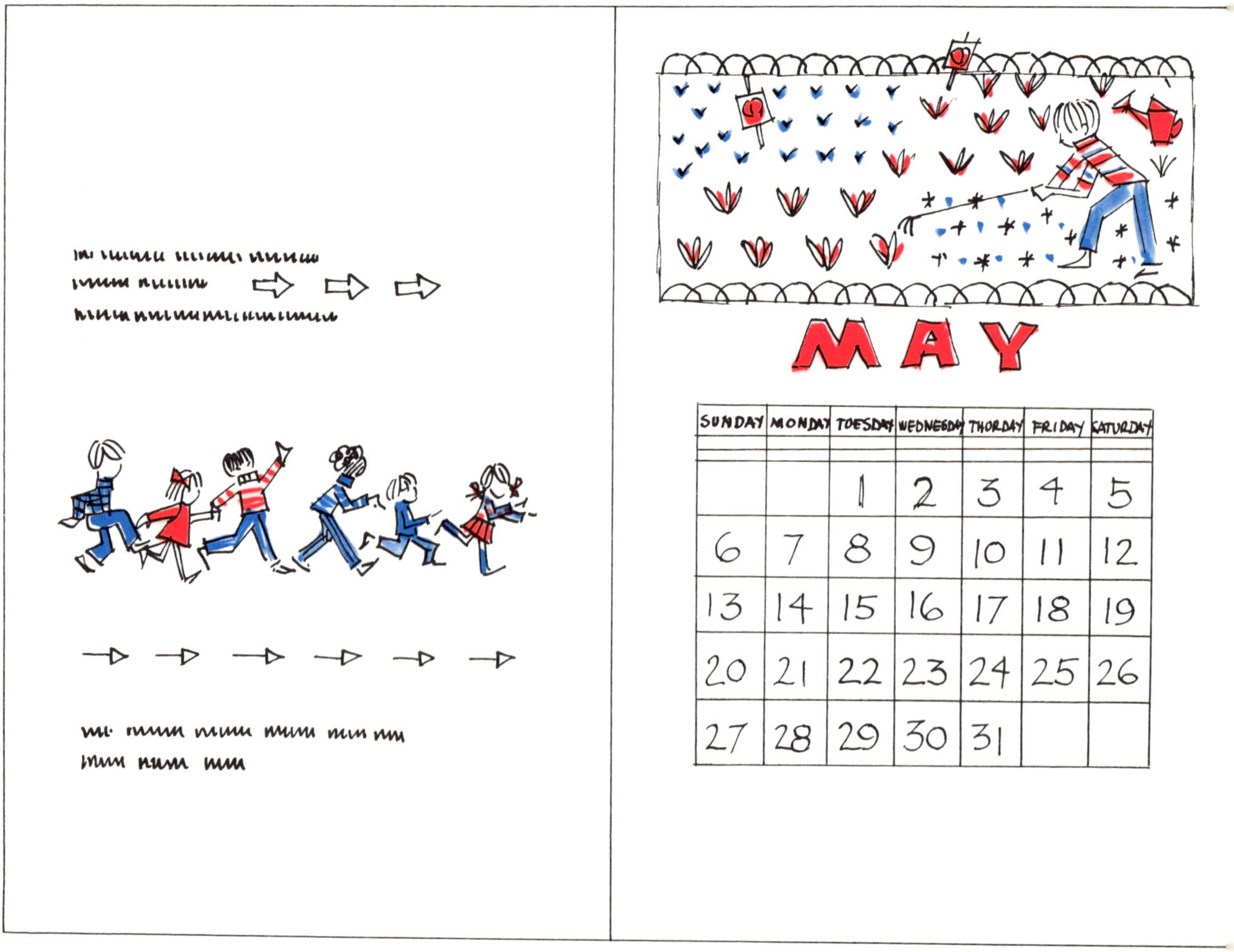

LEFT SIDE

RIGHT SIDE

Every page has a left side and a right side.

This is the left side of the page.

This is the right side of the page.

These words go *across* the page from left to right.

  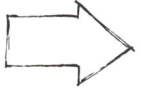 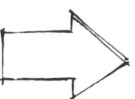 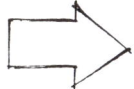

In school you learn to read and write
across each page from left to right.

Look at the room on the left side of the book.
Is the door on your left or on your right?
Where is the window?
Where is the bed?
Where is the fish bowl?
Where is the lamp?
Where is the toy box…
the chest of drawers…
the book case?

In this classroom find a boy with his right hand in his pocket.
Is the girl sitting at the table leaning on her left hand or her right hand?
Is the boy drawing at the table left-handed or right-handed?
What about the girl painting at the easel?
Through the window you can see children in the playground. Are they walking toward the right or toward the left?

To help you remember left and right,
you can make special mittens.

You will need two pieces of felt in one 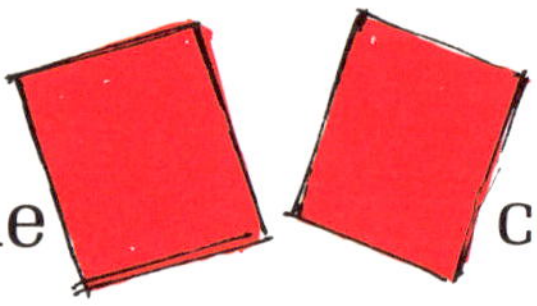 color, and two pieces of felt 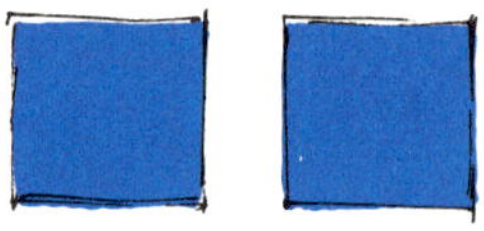 in another color.

You will need scissors, 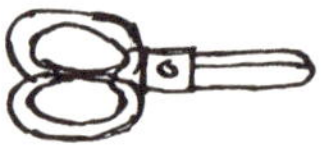 a felt-tipped marker,  and a  tube of cement.

On two pieces of felt the same color,
trace around your left hand with the
felt-tipped marker. With the scissors,
cut the shapes a little larger than the lines
you have traced. Now you have the top and
the bottom of a mitten for your left hand.

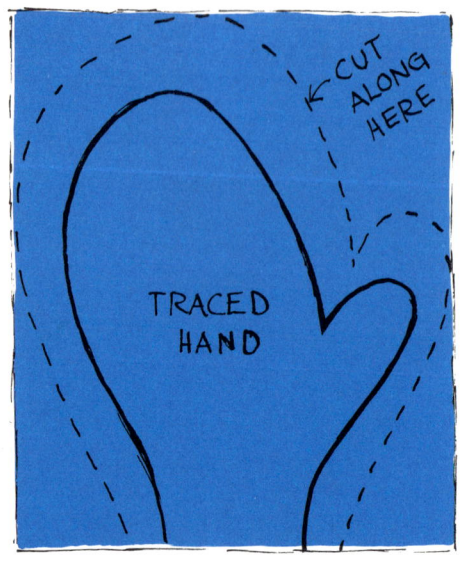
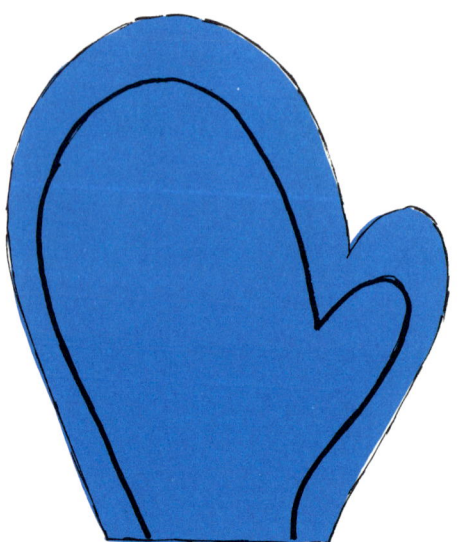

Squeeze cement out of the tube along the
curved edge of one part of the mitten.

Place the second part of the mitten on top over
the cement and allow both parts to dry together. With
the marker, make a big "L" on the top of the mitten.
"L" is for *left*.

Trace around your right hand on the other pieces of
felt. Then cut and paste. Make a big "R" on the
top of the finished mitten. "R" is for *right*.

Now that you have a mitten for your right hand and a mitten for your left hand, you are ready to do the Hokey Pokey.

First you put your right hand out in front of you.

Then you put your right hand behind you.

You put your right hand in front again and shake, shake, shake.

You do the Hokey Pokey by putting both hands up in the air and shaking them while you turn all around.

Then you start all over again with your left hand—
and after that, you begin again with both hands.

THE HOKEY POKEY

Continue as above...

Right foot, left foot, both feet.
Right shoulder, left shoulder, both shoulders.
Right hip, left hip, both hips.
Whole self.

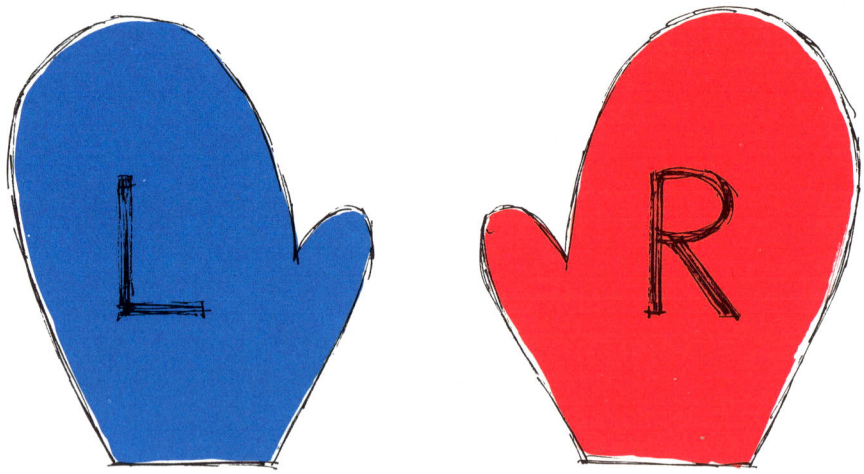

NOTE:

As a step toward reading readiness preparation, the young child must recognize the difference between left and right. In this book we have employed color as a visual aid. *Left* is represented by blue and *right* is represented by red in the mittens worn by the children. We have attempted to illustrate how the understanding of this concept can be fortified and reinforced at home and in the classroom situation by means of simple exercises and comprehension testing that make learning fun.